Miracles Happen™

The Saving Lillian Bay Story

By Ron Knight

Featuring Lillian Bay Beatty

When Lillian Bay was at All Children's Hospital on her first Christmas night, two other children in nearby rooms had died. We do not know their names, but we dedicate this book to those children, along with every other child that needs a miracle today.

Miracles Happen™

The Saving Lillian Bay Story

By Ron Knight

Featuring Lillian Bay Beatty

This is the story of Lillian Bay . . .

Her troubles began way before she was even born. A doctor said that Lillian had a black spot on her throat and he was not sure what the black spot was, or how to make it better.

The doctor then said to Lillian's parents, Brad and Nikki, "There is a good chance your child will not survive after she is born."

Of course, Brad and Nikki took the news hard. They cried like never before, knowing that their unborn child needed a miracle.

Brad and Nikki did not give up. They went to more doctors and asked everyone they could for help. It seemed like every doctor visit brought more bad news.

One doctor said, "I'm sorry, but I do not know what to do."

Another doctor said, "I've never seen this kind of problem before."

"Her chances are not good," another doctor told them.

Brad and Nikki lowered their heads, tears drizzling from their eyes. They did not want to believe that their baby would never be born. They just wanted Lillian to have a chance, even if it was just a small chance. But what could they do?

Brad and Nikki decided to fix up the baby's room. They painted it pink, added a crib, and filled the room with baby toys and stuffed animals.

They believed that someday their baby would come home. The baby would become a little girl and draw pictures to put on the walls, play with the toys, and love her stuffed animals.

Two months later on November 11th, 2009, a miracle arrived. Lillian Bay was born!

♥

Message from Lillian Bay…

"A miracle will happen today.
You just have to keep believing."

Helpful Doctors

After Lillian Bay was born the doctors discovered that she had a disease called Cystic Hygroma. It causes her tongue and throat to be swollen and created a large growth on her jaw. Doctors are still learning about Cystic Hygroma and still trying to find ways to treat babies that are born with the disease.

It was impossible for Lillian to breathe, so the doctors had to put a trachea in her throat, which is a plastic tube that allows air to go inside Lillian's body.

At a special place called All Children's Hospital, many doctors worked together to help Lillian.

There was a doctor that would have to do surgery on Lillian to find ways to get rid of the disease.

Lillian needed a different doctor to take care of her ears, nose, and throat.

There was a doctor that put a feeding tube inside Lillian's belly because it was difficult for her to drink a bottle, or eat baby food.

Another doctor helped Lillian with her breathing.

A doctor helped Lillian communicate since she could not speak.

A doctor took care of Lillian's fragile and damaged skin because of all the tubes, wires, and bandages.

There was a doctor that would treat Lillian when she coughed, sneezed, and became even sicker, along with many nurses that stayed close to Lillian and watched her every minute, both day and night.

Brad and Nikki looked at their little angel and said to her, "Someday you are going to get better. We will say that every single day until it becomes true."

♥

Message from Lillian Bay…

"No matter how bad things are today,
believe in the power of someday."

Dreaming

Lillian was in her hospital bed very, very, weak. Brad leaned down and whispered in his daughter's ear, "Keep breathing honey. Keep trying. You are such a strong little girl."

With her eyes closed Lillian could hear her father's voice. Then Lillian drifted into a deep sleep. She began to dream of so many wonderful things.

Blue sky.

Warm ocean.

Playing on the beach.

A cool sea breeze.

Lillian dreamed that she was smiling and laughing.

Suddenly, Lillian heard another voice. "She is so pretty," her mother said.

Lillian wanted to open her eyes but could not. Instead, she kept on dreaming.

She was painting.

Playing in a pink room.

Hugging a teddy bear.

Dancing to music.

Dreams are special to Lillian because they took her away from her problems. She could transform into any person or go to any place.

Lillian dreamt about riding around in a golf cart and everyone waving to her and yelling, "Hi Lillian Bay!"

Even as a baby Lillian had decided to try really hard to make all of her dreams come true.

Lillian felt her mother and father holding her tiny fingers. Her mother sang a wonderful song. Lillian was so happy even if her parents could not see her smile.

♥

Message from Lillian Bay…

*"If you are having trouble opening your eyes,
then you should keep on dreaming."*

Pictures

Still just a baby, Lillian opened her eyes while in the hospital room. At first she thought that she was still dreaming, but this was real. Lillian's mother held her, rocking her back and forth.

Lillian looked around and saw her daddy. He had a really big smile on his face.

She kept looking around, seeing pictures of people all over the hospital room. Her mother said, "These pictures are of your family and friends."

Lillian smiled. She could not wait to meet all these people. Then she saw a strange picture; a dog that looked like it was made of chocolate.

"That is our family pet," her dad said. "Her name is Hannah."

Lillian giggled. How funny it was to have a chocolate dog named Hannah.

Every picture reminded Lillian of all the family and friends that were anxious to meet her. The photographs showed Lillian a world outside of the hospital room.

♥

Message from Lillian Bay…

"Pictures remind us of all the
people that love you so much."

Fire Truck

Lillian's father, Brad, is a UPS driver that works on an island called Boca Grande, which is a small town in Florida. While Lillian was in the hospital Brad still had to work, so he drove his big brown truck around the island and delivered packages.

The firefighters on Boca Grande wanted to do something special for Brad, Nikki, and Lillian so they bought a ton of presents and loaded them into the fire truck.

Then they turned on the siren, flashed the lights, and drove around the island looking for Brad. When they found Brad, the firefighters jumped out of the fire truck and loaded the presents inside Brad's brown truck.

Firefighters are so important to our community. They risk their lives everyday to save others. Sometimes a fire can occur in the middle of the night, or while the firefighters are eating dinner, or watching a movie. No matter what they are doing, if the bell rings, they are prepared to put out fires and save lives.

The most amazing thing about firefighters is that they run into places that people are running away from. In times of trouble they are heroes.

Brad was so thankful for what they had done for his family. He finished delivering all the boxes in his truck. Then, he drove to the hospital and delivered the presents from the firefighters to Nikki and Lillian.

♥
Message from Lillian Bay…

"The next time you see a fireman, make sure you say, 'Thank you for protecting us!'

And the next time you see someone in a big brown UPS truck, you should yell, 'GO BROWN!'"

Miracle Magnet

Lillian and Nikki were still at All Children's Hospital. Brad thought about his family at the hospital, wishing that he could be next to them right now, but he had to keep working and deliver boxes to everyone on Boca Grande.

One day after Brad delivered a box to a customer he hurried back to his brown UPS truck and noticed something on the floor. It was shiny and beautiful and it spoke to him.

It was a magnet.

Brad leaned down and picked up the magnet from the floor. "How did it get here?" he wondered.

There were two important words on the magnet that changed Brad's life.

"Miracles Happen!"

♥

Message from Lillian Bay…

"Do you know what a miracle is?
If not, then hurry to a
mirror and take a good look!"

Going Home

When Lillian was two months old, the doctors decided she could go home. Brad and Nikki were nervous about taking Lillian home because she was still so very ill with the disease. Lillian's parents only felt safe inside the walls of All Children's Hospital, where they took such good care of her.

Now it was their turn to take care of Lillian.

The trip would take about two hours. Lillian was in the backseat with her mother while her father drove.

What if the tube in Lillian's neck that helped her breathe suddenly clogged up? What would dad and mom do? What if they got into an accident on the way home?

They drove over a big yellow bridge that was so high that the boats down below looked like tiny ants. They were getting farther and farther away from the hospital while getting closer and closer to home.

After the long drive they finally arrived home, safe and sound. Greeting them was their chocolate dog, Hannah, who wanted to give everyone chocolate kisses.

They took Lillian to her bedroom and laid her down gently in the crib.

This was a great moment for Lillian. Her illness started long before she was born. Brad and Nikki thought about when doctors said that

Lillian might not survive.

But here she was…safe at home!

♥
Message from Lillian Bay…

"Do not think about things that can go wrong.
Instead, think about everything that can go right!"

Bedroom

While in her crib, Lillian looked at her bedroom. It had pink walls with pretty pictures. There were many toys, books, stuffed animals, and tons of pretty clothes and a white rocking chair.

Also there were many wires, machines, and medicine to help Lillian. Special nurses stayed at the house and took extra care of her. She met so many family and friends that loved her very much.

Lillian was proud of her bedroom and could not wait until she could walk around and play with the toys and stuffed animals, read the many books, and paint more pictures to go on the walls.

♥

Message from Lillian Bay…

"Your bedroom can be the most special place in the world."

Spaghetti Dinner

When Lillian was three month's old, the Cystic Hygroma disease had become worse. The growth on her tongue, mouth, and throat began to swell even more. Her lungs were congested with fluid and the trachea in her throat that was supposed to help Lillian breathe kept getting clogged.

To make things even worse, her parents needed more money for Lillian's expensive medical care.

All the people on the Boca Grande Island came to the rescue. They held a spaghetti dinner to raise money to help Brad and Nikki take care of Lillian.

A newspaper called the Boca Beacon wrote a story about Lillian and asked that everyone show up to the spaghetti dinner. A group of people baked pies and tasty desserts.

385 adults and 23 children showed up to the event!

Also, students and teachers from Island School on Boca Grande attended the fundraiser. The principal said, "It's so important to help every family that lives and works here, especially when the help is needed for a child."

$12,000 was raised at the spaghetti dinner to help Lillian!

♥
Message from Lillian Bay…

"Spaghetti, desserts, and love can change a person's life."

Harpoon Harry's!

In the Fisherman's Village, an awesome place called Harpoon Harry's wanted to have another fundraiser to help Lillian Bay.

Someone setup a bright light that goes deep into the ocean, which invites all the fish to carry tons of treasure with them. Local fisherman took kids and adults on their boats to have an exciting adventure. Men and women in brown outfits arrived in big brown trucks. A waitress named Amanda McCorkle donated all the money she earned. And all the people at Harpoon Harry's signed their name on a big skateboard.

The guests danced along with pirates, fishermen, and sailors. There were cool games to play and awesome food to eat.

$13,000 in treasure had been raised for Lillian Bay to help with her doctor bills!

♥
Message from Lillian Bay…

"Your bright light can shine even in a big ocean!"

Palm on the Park!

Despite all the bad news Lillian received from doctors, the many surgeries, and the Cystic Hygroma disease, Lillian made it to her first birthday. What is a great way to cheer up a sick little girl? Dress her up!

There is a fancy store on Boca Grande called Palm on the Park. Inside are many different colored dresses, shoes, and bathing suits. On the front counter is a picture of Lillian Bay wearing a pink dress and smiling at everyone that walks by.

Lillian loves to come inside the store, try on different clothes, laugh, and even play. You would never know that Lillian has a serious illness or has trouble breathing.

Small stores like this are unique because you can buy things that you cannot find in any other store. Lillian's favorite dress is the pink one…

No wait. Her favorite dress is the bright green one…

No wait. Her favorite dress is the pretty blue one with all the flowers.

Actually, Lillian has a tough time choosing dresses in the store because she loves them all!

Like so many other people, the employees at the store wanted to lend a hand in raising money for Lillian's doctor bills. They sold 200 fancy silk scarves and raised $5,000!

The owner at Palm on the Park said, "Lillian Bay is so special. We were so glad that we were able to help her!"

♥

Message from Lillian Bay...

"Choose one outfit that when you put it on, no matter what kind of mood you are in, the outfit always makes you happy."

Bluegrass at Sunset!

Do you know what bluegrass is? (No, it's not grass that is blue.) It is fun music that sings about coal minors, mountains, trains, and things that people do in places like Kentucky and West Virginia.

Bluegrass is like mixing country music, folk music, Irish music, English music, and jazz all into one big ball of fun!

The band members play many different instruments. One plays the banjo, another plays the guitar. There is a fiddle, string bass, harmonica, and the mandolin. A mandolin looks kind of like a guitar shaped like a big teardrop.

At sunset on the beach in Boca Grande there is a bluegrass band. People from all over the island come to hear them play, while dancing, singing along, and watching the sunset with its brilliant colors of oranges, purples, reds, and blues.

Lillian Bay is still growing and loves to join in the fun. She smiles and dances to the music that sounds like:
Boom chucka, boom chucka, boom, boom, boom!

The band members tickle the strings and everyone dances and claps to the music. Lillian leads the group showing people that no matter what kind of illness you have, there is always a way to ***DANCE!***

♥

Message from Lillian Bay…

"Boom chucka, boom chucka, boom, boom, boom!"

Snook Nook!

Lillian and Daddy liked to go to a special place called the Snook Nook. It's a beautiful house with a white picket fence, a charming white porch, and matching white chairs with colorful pillows.

Lillian was now two-years-old and enjoyed visiting the Snook Nook the day before Easter to spend time with friends and a little white dog named Bokie. Lilly grabbed all the pillows and chased Bokie around, then let Bokie jump on her lap.

On a wall at the Snook Nook, Lillian noticed one of her paintings. She smiled and felt a sense of pride knowing that she had become quite the gifted artist.

She then played with puzzles that were given to her as Easter presents and then just relaxed next to Bokie.

The Snook Nook was an amazing place, because it always made Lillian feel a whole lot better.

♥

Message from Lillian Bay...

"A Snook Nook is the only place in the world that problems do not exist. Try to find a Snook Nook in your life."

But some days are hard . . .

Lillian tried to be happy every chance she could but there were times when she was so sick it drained away all her energy.

Just about every week, Lillian had a hospital appointment, or she had some kind of surgery so that doctors could continue trying to rid her of the disease. Nothing seemed to be working but Lillian used all her strength to keep fighting the Cystic Hygroma. The older she became, the harder she fought.

But some days were harder than others.

The doctors and nurses at All Children's Hospital helped Lillian with her breathing, her talking, and eating. These are things that most children can do without problems, but because of the growth inside Lillian's mouth, it was extremely difficult.

The Cystic Hygroma was trying to steal away her life. Lillian trusted her doctors, nurses, mother, father, family, and friends. She decided to keep trying, no matter how much pain she was in.

Lillian was also determined to keep laughing, dancing, and playing. She was going to use her skill as an artist and continue to paint.

Everything Lillian did was the opposite of what the Cystic Hygroma wanted. The disease was part of her life, but she was not going to let it take her life.

♥
Message from Lillian Bay…

"Some days I feel like singing and dancing.

Some days I feel like drawing pictures.

Some days I feel like giving someone a big hug.

But somedays, it is hard to take a breath of air.

Some days . . . it is hard for me to just open my eyes."

Baseball!

Lillian's father was asked to throw the first pitch at a baseball game. She watched as her daddy walked on the field and stood on the pitcher's mound. The crowd was on their feet, cheering and clapping. The baseball team called the Stone Crabs was dressed in their light blue uniforms, also cheering Brad on.

Brad smiled at Lillian while holding the baseball, looking a bit nervous. Sweat dripped down his face because the night air was hot.

Brad wanted to throw a strike for all the people in the crowd.

He wanted to throw a strike for the people on Boca Grande.

He wanted to throw a strike for all the nurses and doctors.

Most of all, he wanted to throw a strike for Lillian.

He took one more glance at Lillian then stared down at the catcher. The crowd became silent. Brad reached back with the ball and threw it as hard as he could.

The ball snapped into the catcher's mitt with a perfect strike!

A burst of cheers thundered from the crowd. Lillian clapped for her daddy and gave him a hug.

Being just over two-years-old, Lillian did not know much about baseball. She watched the players hit the ball and run around the bases. Sometimes they were safe, sometimes they were out. At the end of the game, one team won and the other team lost.

No matter what happened all of them would get another chance to play.

♥

Message from Lillian Bay…

"You will have plenty of chances…do not give up."

Angry Birds!

Two women walked into a Target store named Ann and Amanda. They were not shopping for anything, but wanted to walk around the Target and forget about their bad day.

They noticed this little girl standing next to her father. The little girl looked right at Ann and Amanda and pretended to give them a hug from a distance, followed by a grin.

Ann and Amanda walked up to the little girl. Her father said, "This is Lillian Bay. She learned her own sign language and wanted to give you a hug."

"What else does she like to do?" Amanda asked.

"Well," her father said. "She likes to play the Angry Birds game on my cell phone."

Ann and Amanda suddenly had a different mission. No longer were they going to walk around the store angry. Now they wanted to find an Angry Birds pillow for Lillian Bay!

They hurried up and down the isles. Finally, they saw the Angry Birds pillow, bought it, then handed it to Lillian. She hugged her new gift with all the joy and love she could give.

Ann and Amanda had a different view of life from that point on. No longer would they let a bad day bring them down. No longer would they walk into a store like Angry Birds.

Lillian gave them a gift to be happy…no matter what.

♥
Message from Lillian Bay…

"A gift can be a pillow, a smile, or a hug.
Sometimes, a gift can be all three!"

Aunt Maddie!

When you think of aunts, you think of someone older. Well, Lillian Bay has an aunt named Madison who is only fourteen! Lillian calls her, "Aunt Maddie."

When Lillian was in the hospital, Aunt Maddie visited her every Sunday. Maddie could have hung out with her friends but instead she spent her day with Lillian.

Some people saw Lillian in the hospital bed with wires all over her, bandages, and a plastic tube helping Lillian breathe.

But Maddie did not see those things. She saw Lillian Bay as an angel.

For Lillian's first Halloween, Maddie dressed her up as Tinker Bell. And when Lillian spoke her first words, Maddie was there.

On Christmas, Maddie picked up Lillian so she could place a small angel on top of the Christmas tree. Afterwards, Maddie baked chocolate chip cookies.

This was the first time Lillian tried a chocolate chip cookie. She dipped her fingers in the warm cookie then took a bite. Lillian smiled with chocolate all over her face and said, "More!"

"Sure thing," Maddie said, handing Lillian another cookie. "Here you go my little angel."

Maddie once dressed Lillian up in a glittery dress and took her bowling. Lillian kept score herself and after every game, Lillian yelled,

"I won!"

Maddie watched Lillian run around, paint, draw pictures, and play with stuffed animals. That is all Maddie ever wanted for Lillian to be a healthy, happy, child.

One day Maddie took Lillian on an adventure through a church, a garden, and then around the Island of Boca Grande.

People came up to Lillian and said, "Wow, she is getting so big!"

Maddie would always smile and say, "Yes she is."

♥

Message from Lillian Bay…

"Every kid should have at least one outfit that glitters."

Fireworks!

A special friend felt bad that Lillian and her parents had so many problems. The doctor bills were still coming in the mail and Lillian was still fighting with her disease.

That friend decided to send Lillian's family on a special trip to Washington D.C., so they could watch the fireworks on the Fourth of July.

To make the trip even more special, they were given permission to sit at the top of the United States Capitol building in Washington. It is a place where all of our government leaders have important meetings.

The first boom of fireworks went off, then another. Music played as the fireworks went high into the sky and flashed with brilliant colors.

Purple!

Green!

Red!

White!

Blue!

BOOM!

Sparkles.

Flash. Boom-boom-boom…BOOM!

Sparkles. Flash.

Boom-boom-boom-boom-boom.

BOOM!

Sparkles.

One more flash…

A perfect Fourth of July!

♥
Message from Lillian Bay…

"Fireworks remind people to keep looking up."

Liberty Bell!

Lillian had another surgery at All Children's Hospital in attempt to get rid of the Cystic Hygroma. A few months later, a friend of Lillian's father had a great idea. She called a doctor that she knew at Children's Hospital of Philadelphia and asked if they could help. The doctor said he would try his best.

Lillian and her parents took another trip. This one was important, because it could actually save Lillian's life!

While they were in Philadelphia, Lillian had a chance to see the Liberty Bell which is a symbol just like our American Flag, representing freedom. It is a symbol that as a country we should all work together and help each other.

After the Civil War the Liberty Bell was taken to many cities hoping to heal our country after the war and bring people closer together.

Children would clap, cheer, and shout, "When the bell rings, an angel gets its wings!"

Liberty can mean something different for all of us. It could mean freedom from captivity, burden, or disease. It could be the freedom to make a choice, or to seek wisdom.

No condition, situation, or boundary can limit the joy of who you are.

♥
Message from Lillian Bay...

"Liberty is the freedom to be anything you want to be."

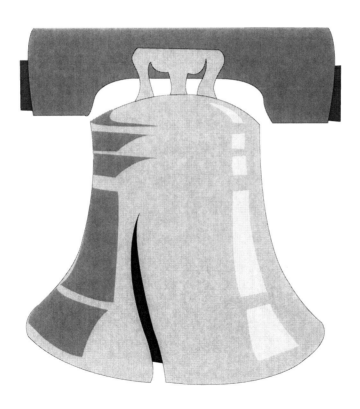

Faith

Do you know what faith is? It's believing in something that you cannot see. It means that you trust everything will be okay.

Lillian had to have faith in doctors and hospitals. Her parents had to have faith as well.

The doctors needed to find a cure for Lillian.

She needed to have yet another surgery.

Lillian still had a plastic tube in her throat called a trachea. It was still the only way she could breathe.

Lillian's parents wanted her to grow up like other children. They wanted her to be without pain and breathe normally.

When Lillian was sad, faith was there for her. When Lillian wanted something, faith always tried its best. If Lillian made a mistake, faith told her to keep trying and do better the next time. On days when Lillian wanted to smile, faith filled her with joy.

Now, it was time to put faith in the Children's Hospital of Philadelphia.

♥

Message from Lillian Bay…

"If you can believe in good days ahead,
it means you have faith!"

Dear Mommy:

You love me so much, even before I was born. You sang songs to me. (Yes, I remember you singing "Somewhere Over the Rainbow!") When you held me, I could see in your eyes how worried you were.

I'm sure it wasn't easy to have a baby with such a bad disease. You cared for me, no matter what was wrong. You drove to the hospital more times than you could count. You stayed by my bed and would not sleep.

With tears in your eyes, you said, "Honey, it will be okay." Even when it seemed like I would not be okay.

I'm sorry that you were so worried, mommy. If I can do anything today, it would be to take your worry away.

I love you...

Lilly

Dear Daddy:

Before I was born, you believed in me. When I was in mommy's belly, the doctor said that I had a bad disease, but you still thought I was beautiful and always knew that I would live.

You did not believe in bad luck. Instead, you believed in me.

You worked so hard and made sure that I was always safe. You watched over me, loved me, and took care of me.

Other kids would go to the beach, so you took me as well. Other kids dressed up for Hallow-een, so you dressed me up. Other kids went bowling, so you took me bowling.

You made sure that no matter what, I was going to be a happy, playful kid.

All the people that helped you from the Island of Boca Grande must have believed in you as well. It made me realize what a special person you are to have so many friends.

One day when I am older, we will look at these words. We will cry, laugh, and remember how many people worked so hard to save my life.

Daddy...I love you!

Lilly

Saving Lillian Bay!

No one likes to see the doctor because that means you are not feeling well. But doctors are important people because they do everything possible to make us feel better.

During Lillian's journey she had to see many, many doctors. In Philadelphia, she saw a doctor that examined the swelling on her face, tongue, and jaw.

Lillian saw a doctor that examined her ears, nose, and throat.

Finally, she was examined by Dr. Jacobs who was a surgeon. This was the doctor that would try to come up with an answer to get rid of Lillian's disease.

Dr. Jacobs also wanted to find a way to remove Lillian's trachea so she could breathe through her nose and mouth. He wanted to find a way that she could eat like any other child.

After examining Lillian, Dr. Jacobs asked to speak with Brad and Nikki. He smiled at them and said, "I think we can help her."

♥

Message from Lillian Bay…

"Keep trying until you receive the answer that you are looking for."

Giggle Juice!

When Lillian arrived at the Children's Hospital of Philadelphia, she was given a secret potion called, "Giggle Juice."

About twenty minutes after Lillian drank the Giggle Juice, she formed a grin, then laughed.

What was she laughing at? What was so funny? Everything was funny! The room spoke in a deep, silly voice. Her mother and father looked weird. And the hospital bed tickled her.

The reason a nurse gave Lillian the Giggle Juice was so she would not be nervous about having surgery, which of course, can be a scary thing to go through.

As for Lillian, she already had over twenty surgeries, but this one was going to be the most important. This would be the surgery that could save her life!

So while Lillian waited, she stood on her bed, held by her mother and father, and giggled.

♥
Message from Lillian Bay…

"All of us should giggle more each day."

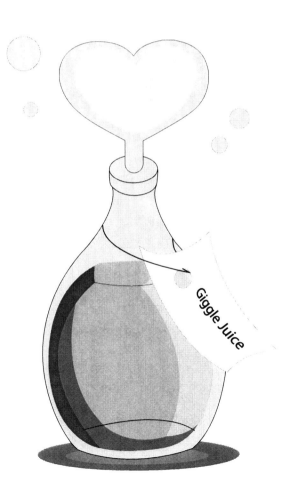

Hope Lives Here!

The two most important hospitals for Lillian were All Children's Hospital and Children's Hospital of Philadelphia. The nurses and doctors were special because they help children overcome sickness, disease, and problems that other hospitals cannot cure.

Each hospital had its own motto.

All Children's Hospital: "Creating healthy tomorrows…for one child…for all children!"

Children's Hospital of Philadelphia: "Hope lives here!"

The only real thing Lillian's parents, family, and friends could do was hope that this surgery would finally work. They wanted Lillian to have a healthy tomorrow.

In fact, they wanted Lillian's story to give hope to all children that are having their own difficulties.

After Lillian's surgery, Brad and Nikki spoke with Dr. Jacobs. In the past, doctors did not have great news to share. Usually, they would tell Brad and Nikki that Lillian had a long way to go with her struggles. But today, Dr. Jacobs said something different.

"Lillian is going to be okay."

Brad and Nikki had been waiting for those words to be spoken since Lillian was born. They did not know if they should smile, cry, or jump up and down. So instead, they kept repeating the words that Dr. Jacobs had spoken.

"Lillian is going to be okay."

♥
Message from Lillian Bay...

*"Create a healthy tomorrow for one child,
for all children! Hope lives here!"*

Healthy Tomorrow's!

The doctors removed 90% of the Cystic Hygroma that Lillian had. They also took out the trachea in her throat, because she could now breathe through her nose and mouth.

Lillian still has swelling in her jaw and throat. Also, a little bit of the Cystic Hygroma still remains, so there is a chance that she could have more problems in the future.

But that does not stop Lillian Bay from believing in a healthy tomorrow.

And it will not stop Lillian Bay from living her dreams.

♥
Message from Lillian Bay…

Family and friends.
Sunday mornings.
Chocolate chip cookies.
Drawing pictures.
Stuffed animals.
Jumping up and down.
Smiling.
Hugging.
Dressing up for Halloween.
Bowling in a glittery outfit.
Placing an angel at the top of a Christmas tree.
Walking in a garden.
Strolling around the block.
Saying hello to people on a perfect sunny day.

May every moment in your life be blessed.

Miracles Happen!

Lillian defied medical odds. She fought through each breath, yet found a way to smile. She fought off the life support machines and found a way to be in peace. She fought through pain, yet found a way to enjoy her life.

If we look back at what had been done through Lillian Bay, then we can look forward, understanding what will happen through Lillian Bay. Her story will be read with tears of hope.

People will say, "Show me the miracle of how a community pulls together with unselfish love to save a child's life."

Others will say, "Show me the miracle of a father that refuses to let his daughter be taken from this world. Show me the miracle of a mother that remained strong for her baby during a life threatening birth."

And even more people will say, "Show me the miracle of Lillian Bay, who did not comprehend strength, love, or faith, and yet, displayed those gifts with each breath."

Today, and everyday, let us enjoy each moment, and know that Miracles Happen…

♥

Message from Lillian Bay…

"I'm not sure what is planned for me in the future, or how my life will be blessed, but I do know something for sure.

This journey is far from over...

Thank you to all the contributors who participated in our Indiegogo campaign to make this possible. A special thanks to:
Customers of Fugates, Fugates, Igrales, Paul Noller, Cynthia Johnstone, Cynthia Bender, Sherry Butler, John Molle, Lisa Arundale, Robert Polito, Mildred Fugere and several amazing anonymous donors. Without your support this project would not have been possible.

To learn more about Lillian Bay and Cystic Hygroma,
please go to www.savinglillianbay.com

For more books by Ron Knight, go to www.authorronknight.com